PARANORMAL
SEEKERS™

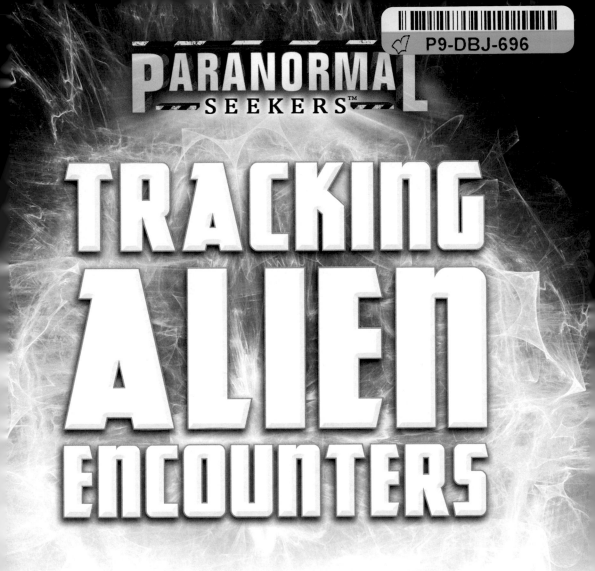

TRACKING
ALIEN
ENCOUNTERS

JENNA VALE AND
JANNA SILVERSTEIN

rosen publishing's
rosen
central®

New York

Published in 2019 by The Rosen Publishing Group, Inc.
29 East 21st Street, New York, NY 10010

Library of Congress Cataloging-in-Publication Data

Names: Vale, Jenna, author. | Silverstein, Janna, author.
Title: Tracking alien encounters / Jenna Vale and Janna
Silverstein.
Description: New York: Rosen Central, 2019. | Series: Paranormal
seekers | Includes bibliographical references and index.
Identifiers: LCCN 2018009641| ISBN 9781508185598 (library
bound) | ISBN 9781508185581 (pbk.)
Subjects: LCSH: Unidentified flying objects—Sightings and
encounters—Juvenile literature. | Human-alien encounters—
Juvenile literature.
Classification: LCC TL789.2 .K475 2019 | DDC 001.942—dc23
LC record available at https://lccn.loc.gov/2018009641

Manufactured in the United States of America

CONTENTS

INTRODUCTION

Starlight falls on a country road in New Hampshire. Headlights speed through the dark as a married couple drives, nervous they are being followed by a different kind of light in the sky. A pilot and his plane disappear after he reports being dogged by an unidentified flying object. Indestructible tinfoil is recovered in the New Mexico desert. Multiple people report being on the Brooklyn Bridge, one of New York City's most famous bridges, and seeing a woman float through the air toward a strange aircraft.

When people think about aliens, they might imagine mysterious gray men with big heads and black eyes, flying saucers with flashing lights, or government conspiracies. The theme song to the beloved TV show *The X-Files* might pop into their heads, or they might shudder as they recall a hand with long fingers clamping onto a young woman's head in the 2017 horror movie *The Gracefield Incident*. The most thrilling and strange stories stick with people for so many reasons, not least of which because they cannot explain them.

In an age when humankind has launched rockets and satellites into space and controlled rovers on Mars, it might seem like people should know for sure by now whether or not there truly is intelligent life beyond Earth. But with everything humans have accomplished so far, they're still learning more each day. Scientists search for water on Mars. Popular science magazines debate the

Accounts of alien encounters are often hazy. People who report seeing or interacting with extraterrestrials usually recall the same basic details, including features such as large heads and eyes, gray skin, and long fingers.

origins of mysterious bacteria on the exterior of the International Space Station. Infrared telescopes and other technologies are developed to aid scientists in their quest for the truth about the universe—people's interest in what outer space holds is simply inexhaustible.

Even though people's understanding of the universe continues to expand, what does that mean for their understanding of strange incidents here at home? Part of learning is making mistakes, running up against limits, and realizing that things might not be what individuals originally thought they were. Stories of alien encounters strongly challenge how people perceive the world, but that doesn't mean learning about them isn't worthwhile.

The more information people gather, the easier it is to make up their minds about what they believe, what they can know, and what they're still not sure of. Were Betty and Barney Hill abducted from that country road in New Hampshire? Where did pilot Frederick Valentich end up if he wasn't taken by an alien ship? Has the government been covering up evidence of extraterrestrials that crashed near Roswell, New Mexico, so many years ago? Whether people can find the answers to any of these questions or not, the stories remain.

CHAPTER ONE

THE AGE OF ALIEN ENCOUNTERS

The twentieth century has been colored by so many fantastic tales of alien encounters, from hazy glimpses of oddly shaped aircraft to actual interactions between humans and extraterrestrials. One such incident occurred on June 24, 1947, and is regarded as the first strange sighting to be widely reported in the United States. Kenneth Arnold, a businessman who was also a trained private pilot, was flying his plane near Mt. Rainier, a large mountain near Seattle, Washington. As he flew, he spotted what seemed to be other aircraft in the distance. Arnold counted nine objects traveling in a V formation and glowing blue-white. He estimated they were traveling more than 1,000 miles per hour (1,609 kilometers per hour).

Arnold described the objects' flight as "erratic" and told a reporter that their flight was "like a saucer if you skip it across water." The reporter called the objects "flying saucers," and the term caught on in the press. In the 1950s, the US government introduced the term unidentified flying object, or UFO, which made it easier to describe unknown aircraft without needing to reference a specific shape. Indeed, a UFO is simply any object in the sky that cannot be identified, so it does not even apply to what might be alien spacecraft. But the association between flying saucers, UFOs, and aliens is undeniably strong, and that's in no small part because of what happened two weeks after Kenneth Arnold saw those objects in Washington.

EXCITEMENT IN ROSWELL

In July 1947, rancher Mac Brazel discovered metallic debris spread over his ranch just outside Roswell, New Mexico. Upset about the garbage, which he assumed was military wreckage, he called officials at Roswell Army Air Field (RAAF), the local air force base. The RAAF issued a statement claiming to have recovered a crashed "flying disk." The local newspaper reported the story, and the news quickly spread around the world. The military initiated a high-security search and cleanup operation. Witnesses who examined the debris reported seeing pieces of metal with symbols thought to be writing and bits of foil that couldn't be burned, creased, or torn.

Soon afterward, the initial press release was retracted on orders from General Roger M. Ramey, commander of the Eighth Army Air Force, now in charge of the investigation. Major Jesse Marcel, who had been handling the research and recovery mission up to that point, stated that the debris was nothing more than the wreckage of a weather balloon. The quick change in the story fueled suspicions that the government was hiding something.

In the years that followed, other strange evidence was gathered. Local witnesses testified that they saw debris they couldn't identify, and firefighters stated they had seen a second crash site where shrunken, burned bodies were found. There were even military personnel who admitted to participating in a cover-up. Was the debris a weather balloon or something else? Were alien bodies taken away for examination? Was there a survivor? The physical evidence collected was reportedly shipped out of Roswell to destinations unknown, and many of the Roswell records appeared to have been destroyed.

Major Jesse Marcel crouches with some of the otherworldly material recovered from the UFO site near Roswell, New Mexico.

The US Air Force has also changed its story several times over the years. In the 1990s, they released follow-up reports saying that the balloon testing was part of a secret program to monitor radiation levels and Soviet atomic activities. They also argued that people's reports of UFO crashes and alien corpses had reasonable explanations: the bodies were actually human servicemen and military crash test dummies from accidents in the desert; or the "alien" evidence was the result of the mistaken memories of people, distorted by time and collected over many years.

CLOSE ENCOUNTERS: SETTING THE TERMS

In 1956, the National Investigative Committee on Aerial Phenomena (NICAP) was formed to study UFO encounters in an objective and scientific manner. NICAP investigated reports made by believable witnesses such as pilots, military officers, and scientists. The US government investigated UFO reports under the code names Project Sign, Project Grudge, and Project Blue Book. These three projects seemed to concentrate on debunking the validity of UFO reports rather than trying to substantiate them. Soon, however, people began to claim that aliens from UFOs had abducted them.

Dr. J. Allen Hynek, who had worked on Projects Sign, Grudge, and Blue Book, founded the Center for UFO Studies (CUFOS) in 1973. Hynek created the term close encounters as a way to classify the kinds of sightings and contact that people reported, and they are defined in terms of increasingly close encounters with alien life. The classifications are as follows:

- The first kind: UFO sightings within at least 150 yards (137 meters)
- The second kind: physical evidence such as burn marks on the ground or unidentifiable materials left at the location of a sighting

- The third kind: sighting UFOs with visible occupants
- The fourth kind: personal encounters with alien entities or abductions
- The fifth kind: actual communication between a human and an alien

There are documented reports of claims for every kind of encounter, with some cases including more than one kind.

"Beaming up" into an alien spacecraft is a popular concept in movies and TV shows that feature alien encounters. What kind (or kinds) of encounter would beaming up qualify as?

Because of the history of conflicting reports, people still debate what really happened near Roswell, New Mexico. What's more, people who were involved in the incident so long ago may feel it's safer to tell the truth now that so many years have passed. For example, Major Jesse Marcel has admitted in recent years that he had no idea what the material they recovered from the crash site was, but he could not attribute it to any aircraft he had ever known. And notably, in 2008, Sergeant William C. Ennis, a flight engineer who was present at the facility when the crash site material was brought in, said that the material came from a spaceship, and he did not know how the ship flew.

MAKING CONTACT

In the aftermath of World War II (1939–1945), everything was changing. The world was seeing the consequences of atom bombs dropped on the Japanese cities of Hiroshima and Nagasaki; the space age was dawning; and the Cold War between the United States and the Soviet Union was on everyone's mind. It was a time when anything seemed possible. The stage was set for people to treat reports of close encounters seriously.

In 1952, when George W. Van Tassel told the world that he had been in psychic contact with "Lutbunn, senior in command first wave, planet patrol, realms of Schare," it seemed too fantastic to believe, but people listened. As many as five thousand men and women flocked to the Giant Rock Interplanetary Spacecraft Conventions that Van Tassel founded, held in the California desert. These conventions continued through 1977 and included lectures, panel discussions, book and paraphernalia dealers, and people who claimed to be in contact with aliens, or contactees, of every stripe telling their tales.

Another prominent contactee was George Adamski, a Polish immigrant to the United States. Adamski claimed, beginning in the late 1940s, to be in regular contact with people from Mars, Venus, and Saturn. He referred to these people as Space Brothers. Described as tall, remarkably humanlike, and very good looking, the Space Brothers had only one message: humanity should abandon its warlike ways, stop the coming nuclear holocaust, and enter an era of peace and abundance called the Cosmic Age.

Adamski wrote four books on the subject. His

George Van Tassel poses before his Integratron near Giant Rock, California, in 1962. The banner above him bears a description of what the Integratron can accomplish—certainly a tall order.

second, *Inside the Space Ships* (1959), detailed several meetings with the Space Brothers. Adamski wrote that sometimes he was compelled to drive into Los Angeles and check into a hotel. Once there, he would go to the bar and be greeted by tall, handsome people who would escort him to their small, saucer-shaped scout ship, which was hidden in the desert. They would then fly off to the mother ship and take him to see the far side of the moon, where thriving cities shined in the darkness. As proof of his contact with the Space Brothers, Adamski presented photographs and home movies of the ships he claimed to encounter and diagrams of the ship interiors.

Expert examination, however, showed the photos and movies to be hoaxes, models suspended on fishing wire. Though Adamski's message of peace was still timely, the weight of evidence against him was overwhelming. With no atmosphere or water source, for example, the moon harbors no sparkling cities on its dark side.

THE TRUTH IS OUT THERE

In the 1970s, another contactee came to prominence. Eduard Albert "Billy" Meier, a Swiss farmer, said he was contacted telepathically by visitors from the Pleiades, a cluster of stars. These beings traveled in crafts called beamships. The visitors said he was selected to be a "truth officer" to learn what they had to teach and told him to prepare for a difficult life because he would not be believed. Ultimately, Meier claimed, he developed a relationship with a beautiful blond Pleiadian called Semjase. He kept copious notes of their conversations and presented physical evidence he said was of Pleiadian origin. The most compelling aspect of Meier's story was his remarkable photographs of the beamships. They were crisp, clear images of flying saucers soaring over sunny Swiss mountainsides. There was only one problem: it was all a little too perfect.

Experts were never allowed to look at the original photographs or the negatives. Evidence, such as

There have been many fake photographs of flying saucers in the sky over the years. Meier's photos, similar to the one seen here, eventually did not hold up to scrutiny.

metal fragments purported to be part of a beamship, somehow disappeared. Years later, after their divorce, Meier's former wife, Kalliope, denied that any of the story was true.

It's doubtful that any contactee actually had a close encounter of the fifth kind. Their stories left a legacy that would become a mixed blessing to the study of UFOs: a dispute between skeptics who were wary of bizarre contactee tales and the open-minded, who would be astonished at the next generation of alien abduction accounts.

CHAPTER TWO

THE HILLS AND BEYOND

As intriguing as spying a UFO in the distant sky might be, it would be extraordinary—and no doubt unsettling—to encounter alien life even more closely. Although people will never know how many countless experiences individuals have had that cannot be explained, there are many standout stories like the Roswell incident that shape how people think about alien encounters. After the crash in the New Mexico desert, there was the alleged abduction of Betty and Barney Hill.

HEAD FOR THE HILLS

On the night of September 19, 1961, the Hills were driving south through the White Mountains in New Hampshire. It was a crisp, clear night, good for seeing the stars that swept thick and bright over the landscape.

Suddenly, Betty noticed a very bright star. It seemed to be following them. They stopped along the side of the road several times to try to figure out what they were seeing. Through their binoculars, Betty and Barney saw a cigar-shaped craft, a kind of airplane without wings. Around its edge, it had lights blinking in green, blue, red, and yellow. Betty insisted that no aircraft moves that way, but Barney wanted to believe it was something he could understand: a small, strangely quiet airplane. The truth was that Barney didn't know why, but there was something wrong with that light. Stars didn't move like that; satellites moved in only one direction; and regular airplanes couldn't maneuver in such a silent, jerky, mechanical fashion.

When they stopped again, Barney got out of the car and started walking toward the light. Through the binoculars, he saw a pancake-shaped ship with a double row of windows around its edge. In the windows, he saw

Betty and Barney Hill, seen here with their dachshund Delsey, gained media attention for their story of encountering extraterrestrials in rural New Hampshire.

small figures moving back and forth. One of them was staring right at him. Betty yelled at him to come back to the car. Terrified, he ran, got into the car, and they sped away. Suddenly he and Betty heard an electronic beeping coming from behind. The car shuddered, and they felt a strange tingling, a sudden drowsiness, and then nothing.

When the Hills arrived home, it was just after 5:00 a.m., two hours later than they had expected. They felt nervous and were unable to remember parts of their drive. They both remembered the beeping sound, and they both remembered a point in the trip when they were suddenly 35 miles (56 km) farther along the road than they'd been a moment before. What had happened in between, however, was a mystery.

Betty reported their sighting to the Air Police at nearby Pease Air Force Base. She wrote letters to UFO experts at NICAP. She cajoled Barney into returning to the places where they'd seen the craft, no matter how uncomfortable they both found doing so to be. Ten days after the sighting, Betty had a strange nightmare five nights in a row and then never again. There was also the matter of the missing time. Why had it taken them two extra hours to get home?

DIVING INTO THE MIND

Two years passed. Barney developed ulcers and anxiety so acute that it interfered with his work. Finally, the Hills conferred with Dr. Benjamin Simon, a Boston psychiatrist

The aliens the Hills said they encountered might have looked like the one depicted here. An artist rendered this drawing based on the accounts they provided while under hypnosis.

who used hypnotherapy in his practice. In the doctor's office, under hypnosis, the two hours of missing time were revealed.

In chilling detail, Barney recalled a strange group of men stopping him and his wife along the road. In particular, he remembered the leader's eyes. Barney cried out, "His eyes were slanted. Oh—his eyes were slanted!" He added, "I've never seen eyes like that before." Barney described how the men escorted them through the woods to the ship he'd seen in the sky. He and Betty were taken to separate rooms inside the ship. There, he underwent an intimate and upsetting physical examination. When the exam was finished, he and Betty were returned to the car and sent on their way. Simon recorded all of Barney's hypnotic sessions and planted a suggestion that Barney wouldn't remember the sessions until he was prompted. Simon then hypnotized Betty to see what she remembered.

Betty's tale was similar, though more bizarre. She described a physical examination that included the sampling of hair, skin, and fingernails, along with a painful needle being inserted into her navel. She recalled the alien beings telling her this was a pregnancy test. After the examination, she talked with one of the beings and he showed her a book and a star chart. Finally, she said, she and Barney were returned to the car and watched the ship depart.

In the weeks that followed, Simon worked with the Hills, testing their stories to see if any details changed. He was trying to determine if Betty had planted the abduction idea in Barney's mind, if the story was a hoax, or if it was the result of a psychotic episode. Even details like what had recently been on TV could be crucial in suggesting a narrative to the Hills. However, neither the doctor nor the government experts were able to prove anything. Betty Hill's niece, Kathleen Marden, became the leading expert on the case of her aunt and uncle's experiences. Even though she found discrepancies between Betty's dream and the stories her relatives told under hypnosis, it was still not enough to determine whether or not their recollections were untrue.

The image of the star map Betty recalled stayed with her and she drew a reproduction. It detailed not only stars important to the visitors, but also what were described as trade routes and regular corridors of travel. On April 13, 1965, the *New York Times* published a star chart as part of an article on a new radio source in space called CTA-102. The similarities between the chart in the article and Betty's star map were striking.

ONLY A DREAM?

Betty Hill's nightmare shortly after the Hills' encounter was remarkably similar to the events that she and her husband described separately while under hypnosis two years later. While Betty did mention the dreams to Barney, supposedly he was not particularly concerned at the time, and she did not repeat them to him again. Did she really never mention the dreams to him again in the two years between the incident and their hypnotherapy sessions?

Furthermore, what about the circumstances of their trip? The phenomenon of "missing time" often happens when people are sleep deprived, which the Hills may very well have been as they drove through the night. The human brain is an incredibly complex organ, and people know that their memories are fallible, and sometimes just plain wrong. People's brains want to fill in the gaps when they can't remember something, and that can result in the formation of false memories. It's been scientifically proven that people suffering from sleep deprivation are particularly susceptible to forming false memories without realizing it. If this is the case, the circumstances of the Hills' late-night drive, followed by two years of stress and uncertainty, suggest that maybe the encounter itself was a dream, though not the kind one would expect.

The peculiar pregnancy test was the detail that intrigued investigators most at the time. In the early 1960s, there was no medical procedure that was anything like this. It wasn't until years later that laparoscopy—the practice of inserting a long, thin tube fitted with fiber optics into a patient's abdomen for internal observation and surgical procedures—would be developed and used as a regular technique. How Betty Hill could predict such a development in medical technology remains a mystery.

THE DISAPPEARANCE OF FREDERICK VALENTICH

Whether Betty and Barney Hill were abducted or not, they at least lived to tell the world about their experiences. What about a case in which the abductee never returned?

On the evening of October 21, 1978, a pilot named Frederick Valentich vanished near Cape Otway, Australia, in his Cessna 182L plane. Valentich was not a very experienced pilot, but the weather was good and his planned flight was supposed to last only about an hour. Shortly into his flight, however, Valentich reported that there was an aircraft with four bright lights hovering about 1,000 feet (304 meters) directly above him. It looked so foreign to him that Valentich said bluntly, "It's not an aircraft." Seventeen seconds of silence followed his report, and the transmission finally ended with a disturbing shrieking that sounded like metal scraping against metal.

Valentich was never heard from again, and his plane was never recovered. Some people theorize that Valentich's lack of experience and supposed fascination with UFOs meant that he really wanted to see something out of this world. Instead of accurately assessing his position in the sky, he may have been confused by reflections of his own plane's lights and became disoriented, falling into a "graveyard spiral" straight into the ocean. In 1983, some debris from a plane of the same model that Valentich had flown was found with partially matching serial numbers, suggesting that maybe Valentich had indeed

Frederick Valentich disappeared while flying a plane similar to the Cessna 182 seen here.

plunged into the ocean. However, historian Reg Watson has reportedly found multiple accounts of UFO sightings around the area during the two months prior to Valentich's disappearance. Furthermore, a farmer believed he saw a UFO the morning after Valentich disappeared, and he said Valentich's plane was stuck to its side.

Perhaps strangest of all, about twenty minutes before Valentich disappeared, an amateur photographer took a shot of the sunset in Cape Otway and captured what appears to be a UFO in the sky. Whether Frederick Valentich truly was abducted or simply met an untimely end remains a mystery, but the number of details in support of either case is bizarrely balanced.

COMMUNICATION WITH THE BEYOND

The Hills and Frederick Valentich all kept their eyes on the skies, and others continue to do the same—but sometimes, it takes an ear instead. At the University of California, Berkeley, a research team called Breakthrough Listen is "the largest ever scientific program aimed at finding evidence of civilizations beyond Earth." In 2012, they identified a particular fast radio burst, which is a phenomenon in which bursts of radio signals lasting only a few milliseconds are detected from space. Generally, these fast radio bursts, or FRBs, do not repeat, so finding the source of these bursts and figuring out what they actually are has not been possible.

Because FRBs last only a few milliseconds, satellites can miss them altogether if they're not pointed in the right direction.

The FRB found in 2012, however, has repeated itself multiple times, and new observations reported in 2017 and early 2018 have led researchers to believe that the bursts could be coming from anything from a neutron star to a black hole to alien life trying to communicate across the universe.

CHAPTER THREE

EFFORTS TO DOCUMENT

F rom enthralled family members like Kathleen Marden to large-scale scientific research programs, there have been countless human efforts to document and analyze evidence of life beyond Earth. Astrobiology, ufology, and plain old paranormal investigation are a few of the fields the public hears about when strange incidents occur. Every new case is an opportunity for people in these fields to expand on their techniques and hopefully bring them and others closer to understanding the encounters that contactees have claimed to experience and what they could mean for humanity's place in the universe.

A LEADER IN THE FIELD

By the time that Kathie Davis (a pseudonym, or false name) wrote to Budd Hopkins, a leading investigator in the field of alien abduction, her life was filled with signs of strangeness. She and her mother had scars on their bodies they couldn't explain. There were geometrical patterns in the yard behind her home where grass had stopped growing. She had dreams of gray-faced beings, or Grays, as she called

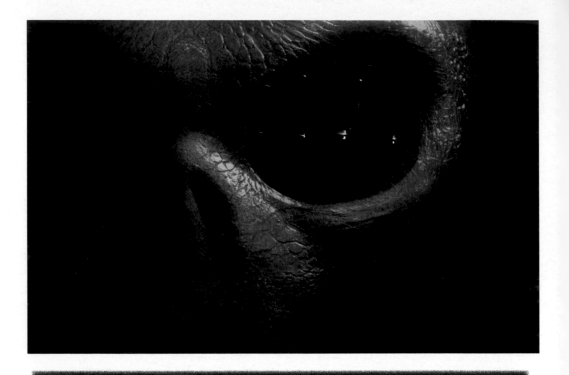

Grays have become the most common form of aliens described by people, such as Kathie Davis, who claim to have encountered alien life.

them, visiting her at night. Her sister, Laura, had experienced periods of missing time. Her mother had seen lights move in and out of the backyard.

Davis wrote to Hopkins after reading his book, *Missing Time*, which described his work and eerily matched much of what Davis and her family members had experienced. Hopkins recognized that everything the Davis family described were classic signs of a possible close encounter. First, Hopkins examined the physical evidence. He had soil samples from the Davis yard tested. The burned soil was chemically identical to the normal soil, but it appeared to have been subjected to extremely high temperatures for a long period of time.

Next, Hopkins investigated Davis's experiences. Under hypnosis, she recalled multiple encounters and abductions that went as far back as childhood. The common element in all of these experiences was the small, gray people, who would meet her and take her elsewhere. She recalled that they had large heads, big black eyes, and small mouths. They seemed to speak to her telepathically.

In late 1977, in the company of two friends, Kathie Davis was in a car when they sighted a UFO. Like Betty and Barney Hill, Davis recalled finding herself paralyzed and taken somewhere to be subjected to an unpleasant physical examination. At the time, Davis was engaged to be married. Shortly after the incident, to her delight she found herself pregnant. Then Davis recalled that just a few months later, in March 1978, she had another encounter that changed everything.

Davis was feeling nervous and unwell, which she attributed to the early stages

Budd Hopkins was a famous American painter and sculptor as well as an active investigator of alien encounters.

of her pregnancy. She started to feel drowsy and then, though she was alone in the house, she felt someone massaging her shoulders and lower back. The experience at first was comforting but then became frightening, as she felt herself being opened up like a flower.

Later, Davis discovered she was no longer pregnant. She hadn't experienced any of the usual signs of a miscarriage, and her physician couldn't explain it. To Davis's thinking, it appeared that the gray beings had taken her baby.

In 1983, Davis recalled, she was abducted yet again. She remembered standing in a room with four Grays. A door opened, and two more Grays came in, accompanied by a little girl with wispy white hair and large blue eyes. She had a small pink mouth, a tiny nose, and a larger-than-normal head for a child her size. One of the Grays told Davis to be proud, that this little girl was part of her, but that the little girl must stay with them. Davis was certain that this was the child the Grays had taken from her. They promised Davis that she'd see the little girl again in the future and then sent her on her way.

Budd Hopkins met a number of other women besides Kathie Davis who told similar stories of having pregnancies that ended prematurely and later being presented with strangely delicate, big-headed children. Other researchers have heard similar stories told by women who were completely unfamiliar with Hopkins's work or the Davis story. Such stories continue to be told by individuals who otherwise seem completely normal.

WHAT SHOULD YOU DO?

A UFO is an object or light seen in the sky or on land whose appearance, motions, lights, and colors do not have a logical or natural explanation. Founded in 1969, the Mutual UFO Network Inc. (MUFON) is an organization dedicated to resolving the mystery of UFOs through the efforts of volunteers. People interested in UFO events participate as investigators, amateur astronomers, and journal contributors. Michael Curta, an associate of the organization, has a list of things people can do if they encounter an unidentified flying object. Some of his tips are:

* Remain calm
* Avoid any hazards
* Record the event
* Get the help of witnesses
* Be objective

For those who would like to share what they have seen with others, they can report the event to a UFO research organization or share the sighting on a website for UFO watchers.

COULD THEY ALL BE WRONG?

Another abductee whom Budd Hopkins worked with closely was Linda Napolitano (who has also gone by the name Linda Cortile). Napolitano claimed to have been abducted from her New York City apartment the night of November 30, 1989. As with other abduction cases, Napolitano said she had undergone a physical examination, but there was something else Napolitano described: the aliens had implanted a small cylindrical object in her nasal cavity.

Multiple witnesses reported they saw a woman floating in a blue light over New York City with three alien beings.

In 1991, she contacted Budd Hopkins—and she had an X-ray to prove the implant really existed. It measured about a quarter of an inch (0.64 centimeters) long and appeared to have curled extensions that could potentially unfurl out of her nose.

Shortly after the X-ray was taken, Napolitano believed the implant was removed in another abduction, and she went to see an ear, nose, and throat specialist. The doctor confirmed that there was nothing lodged in Napolitano's nose, but there was evidence of cartilage buildup that suggested something had been there before.

Budd Hopkins was familiar with stories like Napolitano's, but he was not prepared for what came next.
Eyewitnesses began to contact him, saying that they had
seen a woman floating in a blue light with three beings
in New York at the time of Napolitano's abduction. In
light of this information, Hopkins urged Napolitano not
to speak with the witnesses because their contact could
damage the credibility of their stories that were, as far
as Hopkins knew, independent of one another.

All in all, twenty-three witnesses have gone on the
public record saying they saw Napolitano's abduction take place. Although some have raised suspicion
because they were relatives of Napolitano's or could
have been lying, some were total strangers, and they
maintain they know what they saw. The last witness to
have come forward did so in late 2002, which was thir-
teen years after the famous incident. Though it seems
like it's been a long time even since the last witness
went on the public record, it's possible that more details
of this case, and others, could still be unveiled in the
future. The influential ufologist Budd Hopkins passed
away in 2011, but the work he did on cases like Davis's
and Napolitano's will no doubt continue to inspire other
paranormal investigators for years to come.

INTO THE WOODS

The abduction case of Travis Walton is another
landmark in the history of alien investigation. In
November 1975, Walton and six coworkers were in the

mountainous area of the Apache-Sitgreaves National Forests in northeastern Arizona. As loggers, their job was to thin a section of the forest to allow for faster growth. One evening, as they slowly drove their pickup truck down the winding mountain road, they noticed a bright light in the woods. At first, they thought it was a crashed airplane, but as they drove closer they realized that what they were seeing was no ordinary aircraft. It was a golden, glowing saucer hovering 90 feet (27 m) off the ground.

Walton, the daredevil of the group, got out of the truck and approached the saucer to get a better look. His friends urged him to come back, but he refused to listen. As he got closer, Walton heard a quiet, mechanical whine. Suddenly, the whine grew into an overwhelming roar. The saucer began to wobble. Walton started back to the truck. A dazzling blue-green beam shot out of the underside of the saucer and hit Walton in the chest, lifting him off the ground and throwing him aside about 10 feet (3 m). His body landed on the ground and lay still. Mike Rogers, the driver, panicked. He threw the truck into gear and sped away.

Half a mile (0.8 km) down the road, Rogers stopped the truck, realizing that he'd left his best friend behind. Although all the men were frightened by what had just happened, they couldn't in good conscience leave Walton stranded and possibly injured. They drove back for him. When they returned to the spot, however, Travis Walton was gone. So was the flying saucer.

The following days involved a flurry of activity as the news of Walton's disappearance spread. The local police organized search parties to comb the mountain forests. UFO researchers from a group called Ground Saucer Watch came to take soil samples and readings for radiation, magnetism, and ozone. The police questioned Rogers and the others closely, suspecting murder, kidnapping, or fraud of some kind. Five of the six men passed lie detector tests, clearing them of any crime and confirming their belief that they had seen a flying saucer. Later testing confirmed the truthfulness of the sixth man as well. Suspicion remained. Five days later, Travis Walton suddenly returned.

Walton returned to consciousness on the side of a mountain road and, in a daze, called family to pick him up. He thought he'd been gone for only two hours. His five-day beard growth told a different story. Over

Walton and his fellow loggers expected to be alone while working in the Arizona forest. The remote area was supposed to be accessible only by logging roads—but that wouldn't be any trouble for a UFO, would it?

the next weeks, Walton's family tried to shield him from the press while he recovered. The Aerial Phenomena Research Organization (APRO) and reporters from the *National Enquirer* befriended Walton. These organizations sponsored much of the treatment Walton underwent in the wake of his return. He had a physical, had blood and urine samples taken, underwent hypnosis, and took a lie detector test, which he failed due to stress. Walton later passed a lie detector test with more than a 90 percent certainty of truthfulness.

The Walton case is perhaps the best-documented abduction case in the history of ufology. Seven people all say they witnessed the same thing. Trace evidence from the area in question testifies that something unusual happened there; the evidence is consistent with the findings from other UFO sighting locations. One skeptic, an investigator named Jerry Black, after delving as deeply as he could into the case, couldn't punch any holes in the story. The case is unique in almost every way.

Despite all the supporting evidence, the nature of so fantastic and unnerving a subject makes its possibility hard to accept. Skeptics are still challenging the story. They put forward the theory known as Occam's razor, which states that, all things being equal, the simplest explanation tends to be the correct one. Perhaps the Travis Walton case is the exception that proves the rule. The simplest explanation may be the correct one, but once the simplest explanations are eliminated, the fantastic suddenly becomes possible.

CHAPTER FOUR

IS SEEING BELIEVING?

N o matter what the cause of any fantastic encounter or experience might be, it's clear that people still have so much to learn about any number of phenomena here on Earth. Dr. David M. Jacobs, a retired history professor and the author of *Secret Life: Firsthand Documented Accounts of UFO Abductions,* says, "Even if there is only the smallest percentage of a chance that [the alien abduction phenomenon] is real, we should begin to put energy and funding into studying it because the payoff is so enormous. It demands serious attention."

At the other end of the spectrum was Philip J. Klass, one of the best-known UFO skeptics. Klass was avionics editor of *Aviation Week & Space Technology* magazine and one of the founders of the Committee for the Scientific Investigation of Claims of the Paranormal (CSICOP). Klass told PBS's *Nova*, "If extraterrestrials are abducting earthlings, as is claimed, then it is time to alert the federal government to defend us, for our government to join with other governments to defend this planet ... And if this is simply fantasy, then let's dispel it, let's push it off our plate of things to worry about." He passed away in 2005.

The controversy over the possibility of alien contact and abduction has fostered heated conflict in the press, in books, and at conferences across the United States. Part of the debate focuses on the reason for such abductions: even if one believed such kidnappings were possible, why would visitors from another world be so interested in human beings? One might ask the question in another context: why would humans be interested in dolphins, pandas, or Siberian tigers? Catch-and-release programs for exotic species have been part of regular scientific practice in recent decades. Would alien motivation be so different from that of human beings when the abduction scenario suggests such a familiar study method?

EXPLORATIONS IN PSYCHOLOGY

The stories of those who believe they have been abducted by aliens often have striking similarities. People remember feeling paralyzed and extremely frightened. They report seeing flashing lights, hearing loud sounds, sensing the presence of horrifying intruders, and feeling probing and pain. However, some psychologists say that these similarities are not necessarily evidence that the experiences were real. At the same time, psychologists do not believe that the abductees are necessarily all confused or mentally ill.

Susan A. Clancy, a Harvard-trained psychologist, links these experiences to a condition called sleep paralysis. In this condition, a person can wake up while still par-

Sleep paralysis occurs between states of wakefulness and sleep. People experiencing this phenomenon feel they are awake but are unable to move for a brief period of time, which can be frightening.

alyzed in a dream state. In a 2005 interview with the *Harvard Gazette*, Clancy said, "We can find ourselves hallucinating sights, sounds, and bodily sensations. They seem real, but they're actually the product of our imagination." While she believes that these sensations arise from anxiety and a vivid fantasy life, some people may feel the need to find a different explanation. According to Clancy, those who hold beliefs in the paranormal may find that blaming an alien encounter is a way to explain their pain and distress.

Clancy and other social scientists report that people usually come to these conclusions gradually, over a

period of time. In the book *Extreme Deviance*, sociolo-
gist Christopher D. Bader explains that believers have
often found their way to other people that support their
interpretation of events. For example, they might visit a
therapist with an interest in UFOs or attend meetings of
a UFO support group. These interactions strengthen their
belief that they were truly abducted.

A phenomenon similar to sleep paralysis is known
as accidental awareness. This circumstance refers to

Organizations like Starborn Support in New England offer both group
and one-on-one support sessions for people who believe they have been
visited or abducted by aliens.

the experience of patients who are under anesthesia for a medical procedure and suddenly find themselves awake though unable to move. This incident can cause "trauma memories" to form, which don't attach themselves to specific events, but rather to feelings. In a 2014 article for *Scientific American*, Dr. Anne Skomorowsky writes, "Trauma memories are not encoded as logical narratives, but as globs of sensation. Thus a sensory experience—like seeing a hospital worker in scrubs—can cause an awareness survivor to feel overwhelmed with panic and to relive the sensation of paralysis she suffered through while anesthetized."

Skomorwosky discusses how such an occurrence relates to post-traumatic stress disorder, or PTSD, which many alleged abductees have been proven to have. She even delves back into the case of Betty and Barney Hill—Barney had had a tonsillectomy prior to his alien encounter, and when asked about it, he admitted his experience with aliens had felt similar to his experience on the operating table.

Even though these phenomena might explain some close encounters, Dr. David M. Jacobs has maintained that they cannot explain all, or even most, alien abductions. In a 2006 article in the *Journal of Scientific Exploration*, Jacobs reminds readers, "During abduction events, abductees are missing from their normal environments. Police have been called, search parties have been sent out, parents have frantically searched for their children, etc. ... People are abducted while fully awake, driving a car, gardening, and so forth." Jacobs

SEEING THINGS

Another theory is that alien encounters are nothing more than encounters with individuals' own biology and the geology of the earth. In Canada, researchers are exploring the connection between geological activity, UFO sightings, and reports of alien abduction. When tectonic plates move, rubbing against each other and breaking and changing shape, energy is released (like striking a flint to produce a spark). The theory goes that spots of light described as UFOs are, in fact, energy flashes resulting from plate tectonics. Such released energy might stimulate the brain, specifically the temporal lobe, to produce images and experiences in sleep or unconsciousness that resemble the experiences that abductees describe under hypnosis. Experiments at Laurentian University in Ontario have demonstrated that sensations such as paralysis, the feeling of others in a room, fear and paranoia, and visions of gray, waxy-faced beings can be provoked by stimulating parts of the brain with minor magnetic waves.

states that according to his research, less than half of all abductions take place at night while people are in bed. He argues that one cannot explain away all close encounters as nightmares and false memories.

THE CULTURE QUESTION

Another part of the UFO debate focuses on the idea of cultural contamination. So many people have seen movies like *Close Encounters of the Third Kind* or watched television shows like *The X-Files* that, skeptics say, it's hard to find someone who hasn't been exposed to the idea of abduction or the image of a gray-skinned alien with a big head and large, almond-shaped eyes. Such images, they say, have so permeated American culture that even people who honestly believe they've been abducted can't be considered reliable: they may have dreamed their experiences and unconsciously incorporated popular imagery into their memories. However, many investigators, like Budd Hopkins and David Jacobs, say they always withhold certain details from their publicized cases and keep them confidential. These details, they say, are consistent from case to case, are not found in the movies or on TV, and allow them to recognize a genuine abduction experience.

REEXAMINING HISTORY

Investigators are now examining UFO sightings and alien encounters though the eyes of history, religion, folklore, and sociology. After all, from generation to generation, stories of encounters with strange, otherworldly crafts and creatures survive. Has this phenomenon, then, always been around and is there

The pyramids of Giza are made of millions of precisely hewn, incredibly heavy stones. People have wondered for centuries how they could have been constructed without the aid of advanced technology.

even evidence one can study? The construction of the ancient pyramids of Giza, for example, has often been considered a mystery, and many have posited that the technology to build such structures may have come from alien visitors.

Even as late as the 1890s, with the Industrial Age in full swing and new scientific marvels invented every year, people still told stories of seeing things in the sky. Every society tries to explain mysteries in terms of its own frame of reference. In the space age, the flying

DEBUNK IT!

Remember the Grays that Kathie Davis and countless others have described? Today the public is familiar with this depiction of extraterrestrials because of people's reports of encountering them and also because Grays appear in so many facets of pop culture. But what if there's another reason this version of alien life has seeped into the collective consciousness? In November 2003, psychologist Frederick V. Malmstrom presented a case explaining that memories of seeing aliens may simply be memories of seeing adult faces while in infancy. Later published in a *Skeptic* magazine article entitled "Close Encounters of the Facial Kind," Malmstrom presents some of the following points:

- Up to a certain age, babies cannot distinguish between faces, but they do pay attention to eyes and noses.
- Babies' color sensors are not fully developed, meaning the world appears somewhat gray.
- Astigmatism in infants, which is fairly common, results in a "smearing" effect, and babies cannot accurately assess the size of things.
- These factors seem to create a primitive facial recognition "template," meaning adult faces

(continued on the next page)

(continued from the previous page)

seen at a similar distance would always look the same to a baby up to a certain age.

Using all of this information, Malmstrom had a photo of an adult woman digitally altered to create the sort of blurry, gray face a newborn would often see. The result was certainly alienlike! Malmstrom also suggested that the alien faces people recalled during hypnosis or in otherwise drowsy states came from the same primitive facial recognition template.

saucers move at rocket speed. During World War II, pilots reported seeing "foo fighters," fast-moving glowing objects following their aircraft. The stories from the 1890s, before the age of airplanes, describe the ships as dirigibles. In the ancient eras people did not contemplate aliens flying aircraft from other planets. They did, however, speculate about creatures from the Otherworld sent by the gods. Perhaps yesterday's fairies and demons are today's alien visitors in a different guise.

CHAPTER FIVE

FROM THE SKIES TO THE SCREEN

Separating fact from fiction is an invaluable skill that everyone should work on whenever a fantastic-sounding story is presented as true, but that doesn't mean that people can't also enjoy the story, too. No one knows whether or not aliens are real, but they have certainly captured everyone's imaginations. People's fascination with them has extended not only into science and philosophy, but also into many forms of media and pop culture.

EARLY ALIEN ENTERTAINMENT

H. G. Wells was an English writer who brought some of the most famous science fiction stories to life at the turn of the twentieth century, including *The War of the Worlds* in 1898. It was initially serialized, or published piece by piece in a magazine, and then became a novel. It was also turned into a movie, with the original film released in 1953, and another adaptation starring Tom Cruise in 2005. However, this story of Martians invading Earth has been adapted into other forms, too, such as video

Orson Welles had his own live show on CBS Radio in the early 1940s. Welles and his castmates would perform dramatic adaptations of stories, poetry, and history.

games, comics, a TV show, and the most infamous and unusual radio broadcast.

In 1938, Orson Welles, who would later become an acclaimed actor and filmmaker in his own right, performed a dramatization of *The War of the Worlds* over the radio as though it were a news broadcast. The radio drama was put on by CBS's *Mercury Theatre on the Air*, and newspapers across the United States reported that it induced mass hysteria because lis- teners had believed it to be a true news broadcast informing them of an alien invasion. The panic itself has become the stuff of modern legend, but a 2013 Slate article called "The Myth of the *War of the Worlds* Panic" revealed that the hysteria was most likely exaggerated as newspapers struggled to compete with radio broadcasts as people's primary source of news.

IN THE PICTURES

The evolution of the film industry created another arena for alien entertainment, too. The early 1950s were a rich time for movies about UFOs and aliens. One of the first examples of the genre was the 1951 film *The Day the Earth Stood Still.* In this film, an alien named Klaatu arrives in Washington, DC, in a flying saucer. Although he announces that he and his companions have come in peace and goodwill, the arrival triggers panic and chaos. A nervous soldier shoots Klaatu, but Gort, a humanoid robot, brings him back to life to deliver a message from the Galactic Federation: either Earth lives in peace without further aggression, including in space, or the inhabitants of other worlds who have created Gort and robots like him will destroy it. The movie's themes reflected Americans' fascination with aliens, as well as their political concerns and fears during the Cold War. A remake of the film starring Keanu Reeves, Jennifer Connelly, Kathy Bates, and Jaden Smith was released in 2008.

Following this film, a rash of other movies came out featuring alien invasions. Kids and adults rushed to the theaters in droves to see visions of interplanetary monsters attacking the earth. These films included *The Thing* (1951), *Invaders from Mars* (1953), *Invasion of the Body Snatchers* (1956), and *Earth Versus the Flying Saucers* (1956). These films had a strong influence on the growing ufology movement. UFO skeptics have noted that the stories of contactees such as George Adamski and Betty and Barney Hill often had details that strongly resembled the images portrayed in movies.

ENTER THE TWILIGHT ZONE

In the 1960s, science fiction began to occupy more time on television. Groundbreaking shows such as *The Twilight Zone,* created by Rod Serling, began to draw a wide audience. *The Twilight Zone* was an anthology show that used different actors and plotlines for each episode. The show dramatized riveting science fiction stories by authors such as Ray Bradbury, Richard Matheson, and Charles Beaumont. A similar anthology show called *The Outer Limits* also aired during the early 1960s. Episodes of both shows featured creepy scenarios, including many instances of aliens invading and colonizing Earth. Alien abductions and alien possessions were also common themes.

In turn, these shows influenced the most famous sci-fi TV show of all—*Star Trek.*

Created by Gene Roddenberry, the show hit the television airwaves in 1966. Set in the future, the show presented the exploration of space as an exciting new frontier. *Star Trek* followed the adventures of the crew of the USS *Enterprise*, led by Captain James T. Kirk and Mr. Spock. Part of an interplanetary alliance known as the Federation, the *Enterprise*'s mission was "to seek out new life and new civilizations, to boldly go where no man has gone before." Episodes of the show

"To Serve Man" is one of the most famous episodes of *The Twilight Zone*. The plot seems similar to that of *The Day the Earth Stood Still* at first but ends with a twist characteristic of the hit show.

brought the crew into contact with new alien races or face to face with the menacing Klingons and Romulans. Although the first version of the series ran for only three years, *Star Trek* became a cult classic, generating intense fan groups. In more recent years, movies and new generations of the TV series have been set in this fictional world, including *Star Trek: The Next Generation*, *Star Trek: Deep Space Nine*, *Star Trek: Voyager*, and *Star Trek: Discovery*.

MOPOP

There is a special museum in Seattle, Washington, for pop culture fans of all kinds: the Museum of Pop Culture, or MoPOP. A museum founded in 2000 by Microsoft cofounder Paul Allen, MoPOP is "dedicated to the ideas and risk-taking that fuel contemporary popular culture," which is part of the mission statement on the museum's official website.

The museum features interactive exhibits, events, and special collections from all manner of pop culture phenomena in movies, music, comics, and more. Exhibits have included props, costumes, models, and trivia from such sensations as *Star Trek*, *Star Wars*, and even the work of master puppeteer Jim Henson (creator of the Muppets). They also have multimedia installations in areas like the Sound Lab, where museumgoers can collaborate using real instruments. Sections of the museum have also been broken down into complete genres, such as horror, fantasy, and science fiction. For those who want to have their own close encounter with an alien they've seen on the screen, MoPOP may be their best shot!

MoPOP is a sprawling museum that has hosted exhibits such as *Infinite Worlds of Science Fiction* and *Marvel: Universe of Superheroes*.

SPIELBERG'S HIT FILMS AND ALIENS TODAY

Director Steven Spielberg has made some of the most creative, popular, and highest-earning films of all time. Two of his biggest hits of the 1970s and 1980s focused on the subject of alien-human encounters.

In *Close Encounters of the Third Kind* (1977), Roy Neary, an electrical lineman, is going to investigate a power outage when his truck stalls. He witnesses the lights of a UFO in the night sky and even sustains

Roy Neary, played by Richard Dreyfuss, greets alien visitors in *Close Encounters of the Third Kind*. The aliens in this Spielberg film resembled the all-too-familiar Grays.

a sunburn from them. After this experience, strange mountainlike images and five musical notes keep running through his mind. Roy becomes obsessed with learning what these signs represent, refusing to accept a logical explanation. He leaves home to attempt to learn the truth about UFOs. Meanwhile, other strange events are taking place across the world. Government agents and UFO experts, including a French researcher who believes people can use music to communicate with aliens, are investigating. Eventually, everyone's theories and beliefs are put to the test in an isolated area in the wilderness.

In *E.T.: The Extraterrestrial* (1982), a young boy named Elliott befriends a stranded alien that he names E.T. He hides E.T. from sinister government officials and tries to help him communicate with the aliens who left him behind. Spielberg released a revised edition of the movie in 2002, and the classic film's reach has influenced other movies as well, as viewers of J. J. Abrams's 2011 film *Super 8* can attest.

Contemplating the possibility of intelligent life far beyond Earth is a topic that has fascinated many scientists, authors, artists, and everyday people. Whether or not such beings truly exist and can visit humans from places far away, people will continue to enjoy gazing into the night sky and asking, "Could it be?"

abductee A person who has been abducted.

abduction Commonly defined as the kidnapping of a person for illegal reasons. In UFO phenomena, it refers specifically to the capture, examination, and return of human beings by alien visitors.

accidental awareness The state of being partially conscious but unable to move while under general anesthesia.

alien A visitor from another planet.

astigmatism A common condition in which the eye's curve is imperfect, resulting in blurred vision.

close encounter A general term for a variety of experiences people have with UFOs or aliens.

close encounter of the fifth kind Actual communication between a human and an alien.

close encounter of the first kind A UFO sighting within at least 150 yards (137 m).

close encounter of the fourth kind A personal encounter with alien entities or abductions.

close encounter of the second kind A UFO sighting that results in a scar or burn mark on the ground or the deposit or creation of fragments of unidentifiable material.

close encounter of the third kind A UFO sighting that includes visible occupants.

contactee A person who claims to be in telepathic or personal contact with aliens.

flying saucer A popular term used to describe an oblong-shaped unidentified flying object.

Grays A common name for the most-often described abductor; a being between 4 and 5 feet (1–1.5 m) tall with a large head, gray skin, small mouth, and large, black, almond-shaped eyes.

hypnosis A trancelike state induced by a doctor or hypnotist. This technique is often used to enhance an abductee's recall of hidden memories.

pseudonym A false name or alias.

sleep paralysis A temporary state of being unable to move either when falling asleep or waking up.

Space Brothers Tall, graceful humanlike beings from other planets inside and outside our solar system, described by George Adamski and other contactees as messengers to humanity.

UFO Unidentified flying object. The term coined to describe an object that flies through the air but bears no resemblance in shape or behavior to any recognizable form of conventional aircraft. See also flying saucer.

ufology The study of UFOs and related phenomena.

FOR MORE INFORMATION

Committee for Skeptical Inquiry
Box 703
Amherst, NY 14226
(716) 636-1425
Website: http://www.csicop.org
Facebook: @skepticalinquirer
Twitter: @SkeptInquiry
The Committee for Skeptical Inquiry promotes critical
investigation, scientific inquiry, and using reason to
examine controversial and fantastic claims.

J. Allen Hynek Center for UFO Studies
PO Box 31335
Chicago, IL 60631
(773) 271-3611
Website: http://www.cufos.org
The Center for UFO Studies (CUFOS) is a group dedi-
cated to examining and analyzing UFO phenomena.

Library and Archives Canada
395 Wellington Street
Otawa, ON K1A 0N4
Canada
(866) 578-7777
Website: www.bac-lac.gc.ca/eng/Pages/home.aspx
Facebook and Twitter: @LibraryArchives
Library and Archives Canada provides a database of
around 9,500 digitized documents regarding sightings
and investigations of UFOs across Canada.

MUFON Ontario
1395 Lawrence Avenue West
Suite 20030
Toronto, ON M6L 1A7
Canada
(905) 278-9596
Website: http://www.mufoncanada.com
MUFON Ontario maintains a sighting database. It counts
medical professionals and scientists among its mem-
bership and facilitates access to major research
laboratories across Canada for UFO researchers.

**National Aeronautics and Space Administration
(NASA)**
300 E Street SW, Suite 5R30
Washington, DC 20546-0001
(202) 358-0001
Website: https://www.nasa.gov
Facebook, Twitter, and YouTube: @NASA
NASA's mission is to pioneer the future in space explora-
tion, scientific discovery, and aeronautics research.

SETI Institute
189 Bernardo Avenue, Suite 200
Mountain View, CA 94043
(650) 961-6633
Website: http://www.seti.org
Facebook: @SETIInstitute
This nonprofit organization focuses on exploring and
understanding the nature of life in the universe to
inspire and lead present and future generations.

Carey, Thomas J., and Donald R. Schmitt. *Confessions of the Children of Roswell: Preserving the Story of America's Most Infamous UFO Incident* (Alien Encounters). New York, NY: Rosen Publishing, 2018.

Clarke, Ardy Sixkiller. *Sky People: Untold Stories of Alien Encounters in Mesoamerica.* Pompton Plains, NJ: The Career Press, Inc., 2015.

Friedman, Stanton T., and Kathleen Marden. *The UFO Cover-Up: What World Governments Don't Want You to Know* (Alien Encounters). New York, NY: Rosen Publishing, 2018.

Hammond, Richard. *Richard Hammond's Mysteries of the World: Alien Encounters.* London, UK: RHCP Digital, 2015.

Hoena, Blake. *Can You Survive an Alien Invasion? An Interactive Doomsday Adventure.* North Mankato, MN: Capstone Press, 2016.

Miller, Ron. *Aliens: Past, Present, & Future.* London, UK: Elephant Book Company Limited, 2017.

Rajczak, Kristen. *Investigating Hypnosis and Trances* (Understanding the Paranormal). New York, NY: Rosen Publishing, 2017.

Shea, Therese. *Investigating UFOs and Aliens* (Understanding the Paranormal). New York, NY: Rosen Publishing, 2015.

Terrell, Brandon. *12 Frightening Tales of Alien Encounters.* Mankato, MN: 12-StoryLibrary, 2017.

Towlson, Jon. *Constellations: Close Encounters of the Third Kind.* Leighton Buzzard, UK: Auteur, 2016.

BIBLIOGRAPHY

Associated Press. "UFO Enthusiast Missing After Report-
ing Craft." *Toledo Blade*, October 23, 1978. https://
news.google.com/newspapers?nid=1350&dat=
19781023&id=6hFPAAAAIBAJ&sjid=hQIEAAAAIBAJ
&pg=3318,4275388.

Burgan, Michael. *Searching for Aliens, UFOs, and Men in
Black* (Unexplained Phenomena). Mankato, MN: Capstone Press, 2011.

Carey, Thomas J., and Donald R. Schmitt. *The Roswell
Incident: An Eyewitness Account.* New York, NY: Rosen
Publishing, 2012.

Curta, Michael. "Ten Things You Should Do If You Encounter a UFO." *SFGate*, June 26, 2005. https://www.sfgate
.com/entertainment/article/TEN-THINGS-YOU
-SHOULD-DO-IF-YOU-ENCOUNTER-A-UFO-2659459.php.

Gardner, Martin. *The New Age: Notes of a Fringe-
Watcher.* Amherst, NY: Prometheus Books, 1991.

History.com. "Kenneth Arnold." Retrieved February 15,
2018. http://www.history.com/topics/kenneth-arnold.

Klass, David. *Stuck on Earth.* New York, NY: Frances Foster
Books, 2010.

Kneece, Mark, and Rod Serling. *The Twilight Zone: Will
the Real Martian Please Stand Up?* New York, NY:
Walker & Co., 2009.

Lo, June C., and Pearlynne L. H. Chong. "Sleep Deprivation Increases Formation of False Memory." *Journal of
Sleep Research*, December 2016. https://www.ncbi
.nlm.nih.gov/pmc/articles/PMC5324644.

Malmstrom, Frederick V. "Close Encounters of the Facial
Kind." *Skeptic*, 2004. https://www.skeptic.com/reading
_room/close-encounters-of-the-facial-kind.

Marden, Kathleen. "Dreams or Recall on the Hill Abduc-
    tion Hypnosis Tapes?" Kathleen Marden, 2009. http://
    www.kathleen-marden.com/hill-hypnosis-tapes-vs
    -bettys-dreams.php.
McGaha, James, and Joe Nickell. "The Valentich Dis-
    appearance: Another UFO Cold Case Solved."
    Skeptical Inquirer, December 2013. https://www.csicop
    .org/si/show/the_valentich_disappearance_another
    _ufo_cold_case_solved.
Meers, Sean F. "The Witnesses." *The Linda Cortile UFO
    Abduction Case Home*, March 13, 2012. http://www
    .lindacortilecase.com/the-witnesses.html.
Pooley, Jefferson, and Michael J. Socolow. "The Myth of
    the *War of the Worlds* Panic." Slate, October 28, 2013.
    http://www.slate.com/articles/arts/history/2013/10
    /orson_welles_war_of_the_worlds_panic_myth_the
    _infamous_radio_broadcast_did.html.
Rooney, Anne. *UFOs and Aliens* (Amazing Mysteries).
    Mankato, MN: Smart Apple Media, 2010.
Shostak, G. Seth. *Confessions of an Alien Hunter: A
    Scientist's Search for Extraterrestrial Intelligence*. Wash-
    ington, DC: National Geographic, 2009.
Skomorowsky, Anne. "Alien Abduction or 'Accidental
    Awareness'?" *Scientific American*, November 11, 2014.
    https://www.scientificamerican.com/article/alien
    -abduction-or-accidental-awareness.
Strickland, Ashley. "What's Sending Mysterious Repeating
    Fast Radio Bursts in Space?" CNN, January 10, 2018.
    https://www.cnn.com/2018/01/10/world/repeating
    -fast-radio-burst-frb121102/index.html.

INDEX

ABOUT THE AUTHORS

Jenna Vale is a New Jersey native who has followed paranormal stories all her life. She has visited multiple sites of paranormal phenomena, from the dusty roads of *Weird NJ* fame to the haunted vaults of Edinburgh, Scotland.

Janna Silverstein is a writer, editor, and teacher who has published nonfiction in print and online on a variety of subjects, including books, technology, and travel. Her short fiction has appeared in several anthologies as well as in *Marion Zimmer Bradley's Fantasy Magazine*. She has been watching the skies since her childhood but to her disappointment has never seen a UFO or experienced a close encounter.

PHOTO CREDITS

Cover Apostoli Rossella/Moment/Getty Images; pp. 1, 7, 17, 27, 37, 47 (background) sakkmesterke/Shutterstock.com; p. 3 iprostocks/Shutterstock.com; pp. 4–5 (background) Mordolff/E+/Getty Images; p. 5 Liz Kcer/Shutterstock.com; p. 9 Universal History Archive/Universal Images Group/Getty Images; p. 11 ktsdesign/Shutterstock.com; p. 13 Ralph Crane/The LIFE Picture Collection/Getty Images; p. 15 oorka/iStock/Thinkstock; p. 18 World History Archive/Alamy Stock Photo; p. 20 © Charles Walker/TopFoto/The Image Works; p. 24 Bettmann/Getty Images; p. 26 Bandit Sutthirak/Shutterstock.com; p. 28 adike/Shutterstock.com; p. 29 Gamblin Yann/Paris Match Archive/Getty Images; p. 32 © Mary Evans/The Image Works; p. 35 Historical/Corbis Historical/Getty Images; p. 39 © iStockphoto.com/demaerre; p. 40 © iStockphoto.com/Steve Debenport; p. 44 Waj/Shutterstock.com; p. 48 Hulton Archive/Archive Photos/Getty Images; pp. 51, 53 Photo12/Alamy Stock Photo; p. 52 kerochan/Shutterstock.com; cover, back cover, and interior pages (caution pattern) Geschaft/Shutterstock.com.

Design: Michael Moy; Editor: Megan Kellerman; Photo Researcher: Karen Huang